D0710599

BUILDING BY DESIGN

ENGINEERING
THE LONDON
UNDERGROUND

BY KATE CONLEY

CONTENT CONSULTANT
Michael A. Mooney
Grewcock Chair Professor of Underground Construction &
Tunneling, Colorado School of Mines

Core Library

An Imprint of Abdo Publishing
abdopublishing.com

Cover image: A London Underground train arrives at
one of the system's hundreds of stations.

abdopublishing.com

Published by Abdo Publishing, a division of ABDO, PO Box 398166, Minneapolis, Minnesota 55439. Copyright © 2018 by Abdo Consulting Group, Inc. International copyrights reserved in all countries. No part of this book may be reproduced in any form without written permission from the publisher. Core Library™ is a trademark and logo of Abdo Publishing.

Printed in the United States of America, North Mankato, Minnesota
082017
012018

Cover Photo: Martin Keene/PA Wire/AP Images
Interior Photos: Martin Keene/PA Wire/AP Images, 1; David R. Frazier/Science Source, 4–5, 43; iStockphoto, 7; Three Lions/Hulton Archives/Getty Images, 10; AP Images, 12, 39; Print Collector/Hulton Archive/Getty Images, 14–15; Universal History Archive/Universal Images Group/Getty Images, 18, 27, 45; Ipsumpix/Corbis Historical/Getty Images, 21; Science & Society Picture Library/SSPL/Getty Images, 24–25; Tunnel shields and the use of compressed air in subaqueous works/William Charles Copperthwaite/Google Books, 31; ullstein bild/Getty Images, 32; Central Press/Hulton Archive/Getty Images, 34–35; Hoberman Collection/Universal Images Group/Getty Images, 37

Editor: Arnold Ringstad
Imprint Designer: Maggie Villaume
Series Design Direction: Laura Polzin

Publisher's Cataloging-in-Publication Data

Names: Conley, Kate, author.
Title: Engineering the London Underground / by Kate Conley.
Description: Minneapolis, Minnesota : Abdo Publishing, 2018. | Series: Building by design | Includes online resources and index.
Identifiers: LCCN 2017946939 | ISBN 9781532113741 (lib.bdg.) | ISBN 9781532152627 (ebook)
Subjects: LCSH: King's Cross Underground Station (London, England)--Juvenile literature. | Transportation--Juvenile literature. | Building--Juvenile literature. | Subway stations--Design and construction--Juvenile literature.
Classification: DDC 725.3109421--dc23
LC record available at https://lccn.loc.gov/2017946939

CONTENTS

CHAPTER ONE

UNDERGROUND
PUBLIC SU
PLAZA
Traditional Italian Ice Cream
Traditional Italian Ice Cream
Traditional Italian Ice Cream
Multi Flavoured Ice Cream
ICE CREAM
ICE CREAM
P667 HML

THE UNDERGROUND

A cold, wet morning dawns across London, England. Most people are still asleep. But Dylan Glenister is already at work. He is a train driver on the London Underground. It is the world's oldest subway system.

Glenister is ready for a day of transporting thousands of commuters. But before he can pick up passengers, he must inspect his train. He walks through the cars, checking doors and testing the intercom. When all is ready, he begins his route on the Piccadilly Line.

Glenister and his fellow drivers keep London moving. Every year, they transport

Every day, millions of people descend the stairs into the London Underground.

more than 1 billion passengers. Londoners rely on the Underground to get to work and school. But it is more than just a way to get from place to place. The Underground is a marvel of engineering that has become part of London's identity.

TRAFFIC JAMS

Today's massive Underground system began during the Industrial Revolution of the 1800s. It was a time of great change. Millions of people left their family farms. They moved to cities in search of jobs in newly created factories. These factories used machines to produce goods faster and cheaper than ever before.

Many of the new factories were in London, England's capital. The city's population more than doubled between 1800 and 1850. Daily commuters added to this number. By 1855, approximately 750,000 people took trains into London every day. Trains were not allowed in the city center. Commuters traveled as

The Underground is a vital part of London's transportation system.

far into the city as they could. Then they had to walk or take horse-drawn buses or coaches.

London's narrow, winding streets grew crowded. Traffic jams formed near the city's bridges. Fifty thousand horses pulled the buses and coaches. Horse droppings and frequent rain made the streets dirty and slippery. Traveling from one end of London to the other by horse could take more than one hour.

STOCKTON & DARLINGTON RAILWAY

During the Industrial Revolution, trains were a new and exciting way to travel. In 1825, the world's first public train service began in England. It was called the Stockton & Darlington Railway. The line was a great success. New lines opened across England. They opened the way for the London Underground.

IDEAS

Engineers had many ideas for fixing the traffic problem. One plan called for an elevated train to carry passengers high above the street traffic.

Another plan had train tracks lined by elegant walkways. The entire structure would be enclosed by glass panels. Other plans proposed trains that ran along cables or were moved by air pressure.

Most of the ideas were impractical. Besides, many Londoners did not like the idea of trains running through the city. They feared the trains would be loud, ugly, and dirty. But a lawyer for the city of London had another idea. Charles Pearson suggested running a train under the streets.

Pearson's idea had many benefits. The trains would be hidden from view. Their noise would be contained within the tunnels below. And the streets above the trains could remain open to traffic. It seemed like a perfect solution. But no one had ever tried to build a railroad under a major city before.

THE UNKNOWN

In 1854, London's lawmakers approved plans for an underground railway. It would be the first of its kind

in the world. Many Londoners had doubts about the plan. They imagined all kinds of awful events. Tunnels might collapse. Fumes from the trains might make passengers sick. Buildings might shake as trains passed below.

These attitudes changed on January 10, 1863. On that day, the Underground opened to the public. Thirty thousand people rode it. A few days later, new trains had to be added to keep up with the demand.

PERSPECTIVES

"AN INSULT TO COMMON SENSE"

Traveling underground seemed dangerous and unpleasant to many people. In November 1861, the *Times* of London referred to the underground railway as "an insult to common sense." It went on to suggest that riding on it would be "awfully suggestive of dark, noisome tunnels buried many fathoms deep beyond the reach of light or life; passages inhabited by rats, soaked with sewer drippings, and poisoned by the escape of gas mains."

Trials of a train powered by air pressure were carried out on a 600-yard (550-m) test track near London.

Work began on New York City's subway system in the early 1900s.

The railway that had at first seemed dangerous was now a roaring success.

Soon, cities across Europe and the United States began building their own underground railways. Each city's system was different. But they all relied on the pioneering work of the London Underground's engineers. The skill and daring of these engineers created a new age of transportation.

STRAIGHT TO THE
SOURCE

In 1846, a Royal Commission in London met to solve the traffic problem. Charles Pearson spoke to the commission about his idea of an underground railway:

I propose that the [railway] site shall serve the double purpose of a railroad in the basement of six lines, and a carriage-road on the super-surface. I propose it to be constructed, two lines under the two arches in the centre. . . . By using the same site for the double purpose of a street above and a railroad below, I acquire two profits; first, the profit of the railroad; and, secondly, a large return in the shape of frontages for ground-rents; besides this, there is the important benefit which the public will derive from the surface accommodation.

Source: *Minutes of Evidence Taken before the Commissioners Appointed to Investigate the Various Projects for Establishing Railroad Termini. London: W. Clowes and Sons, 1846. Google Books. 137–138.*

Point of View

Members of the Royal Commission were slow to accept the idea of bringing trains into London. What is Pearson's point of view on the issue? In what ways does he attempt to change their minds? Give specific examples from the passage to support your answers.

PLANNING THE UNDERGROUND

Lawmakers approved a site for the Underground that was 3.5 miles (5.6 km) long. It would run from west to east and have seven stations. All the construction work would take place right under the feet of Londoners. Civil engineer John Fowler led this massive project. Fowler and his team of engineers had to look at many factors before building could begin.

The site's soil was one of the first elements engineers studied. Most of London's soil is stiff clay. Its qualities made digging a tunnel under London possible. Clay is impermeable.

London's crowded streets made it clear that a new transportation solution was needed.

DESIGNED BY NATURE

The idea of an underground railway seemed unrealistic to many Londoners at first. And it may well have been, if London had not had ideal conditions for it. Railway manager Granville Cunningham commented on this idea in 1908. He said, "It seems that the beautiful homogenous clay of London has been designed by nature for the very purpose of having tunnels pierced through it, and it would be a great pity to balk nature in her design."

This means that water does not pass easily through it. This quality helps keep the tunnels dry.

Engineers like building tunnels in stiff clay for another reason, too. It does not cave in on itself quickly after a tunnel is dug. This quality is known as stand-up time. Sandy soils have a short stand-up time. They collapse quickly, like a sand castle hit by a wave. Firm soils and rock have a long stand-up time. London's clay is a firm soil, an ideal material for tunneling.

DIVERTING SEWERS, GAS, AND WATER

Engineers had to think about what lay under the city streets, too. Sewer tunnels and pipes posed the largest problem. Years earlier, engineers had covered many of the small rivers that flowed into London. They had made the covered rivers into the city's sewers.

The planned subway line crossed these sewers in several places. Engineers had to figure out how to fit both the train tunnels and the sewers underground. They diverted the sewers to new routes. This allowed the tunnels to pass over, under, or next to the sewers.

Water and gas pipes were also buried below the streets. If engineers hit a gas pipe, a fire or explosion could happen. If they hit a water pipe, a flood of water could spread through the neighborhood. Engineers had to plan their work carefully around these pipes. In areas where the tunnels were deepest, they could build under the pipes. In shallower parts of the tunnels, the pipes had to be diverted.

CARRYING THE LOAD

Engineers also had to plan the design of the tunnel itself. It had to be strong enough to support the moving people and vehicle traffic above it. Engineers call these items live loads. It also had to be able to support its own weight and the fixed weights of roads and buildings, all of which are called the dead load. If the combination of live load and dead load were too heavy, the tunnel would collapse.

For these reasons, engineers chose a tunnel design that had an arch. Its flat bottom, vertical sides, and arched roof looked like a horseshoe. The design had many benefits. The arch could carry a heavier load than a straight beam could. It could support the live and dead loads of the city above. The arch could also span longer distances than a straight beam. This allowed the tunnel to be wide enough for a large train to pass through it. Most importantly, the structure of

Planners had to contend with London's existing underground infrastructure, including sewers.

an arch puts its materials under compression, rather than tension, like a straight beam would. Tension pulls materials apart, and compression squeezes them together. The brick materials used for arches are much stronger in compression than in tension. This gives the arch incredible strength.

A VENTILATION PLAN

Before the trains could run, engineers needed a ventilation plan. Trains released smoke as they ran. This was not a problem outdoors. But in the tunnels, the smoke needed a way to escape. Otherwise, it would remain in the tunnels and make passengers sick.

Fowler had an idea for a fireless engine. It would not release smoke. Fowler's engine worked by putting hot bricks into a water tank. The heated water would create steam. Pressure from the steam would push the trains. But the idea failed. The trains could hardly move.

Engineers looked to a different type of train. It collected steam and smoke in a tank as it ran.

LONDON
UNDERGROUND
CROSS SECTION

This illustration shows a cross section of a London Underground station from the late 1800s. What features discussed in Chapter Two can you recognize? What advantages might this kind of station design have? What disadvantages might it have?

This would prevent smoke from being released into the tunnels. The tank needed to be emptied, so engineers created vents along the tunnels. Trains could empty the tanks as they drove under the vents. Trains could also empty tanks in aboveground sections of track.

With a solid set of plans in place, building the underground railway could begin. It was a risky project. No one knew if it would work. The only way to find out was to start digging.

STRAIGHT TO THE
SOURCE

Civil engineer Sir Benjamin Baker reflected on the pioneering work he and his fellow engineers undertook:

It is known now what precautions were necessary . . . how to timber the cuttings securely and keep them clear of water without drawing the sand from under the foundations of adjoining houses; how to underpin walls, and, if necessary, carry the railway under houses and within a few inches of the kitchen floors without pulling down anything; how to drive tunnels; divert sewers over or under the railways, keep up the numerous gas and water mains, and maintain the road traffic when the railway is being carried underneath; and finally, how to construct the covered way, so that buildings of any height and weight may be erected over the railway without risk . . . from settlement or vibration.

Source: *Proceedings of the Institution of Civil Engineers, v. 81. London: ICE, 1885. Google Books. 26–27.*

What's the Big Idea?

Construction of the London Underground required bold engineering decisions. What kinds of risks did engineers face in planning the Underground? Why might engineers have accepted these risks? What benefits came from doing so?

DIGGING UNDER LONDON

In 1860, work began on the Underground. Most of the line would follow existing city streets. Workers blocked off these streets and diverted traffic to temporary roads. Then work began, using a method called "cut and cover."

The first step was to excavate a large trench. Workers dug the trench by hand using shovels and spades. They created a trench approximately 20 feet (6 m) deep and 33 feet (10 m) wide. It formed the underground tunnel.

The cut and cover construction method was massively disruptive to daily life in the area.

Workers then built wooden frames along the trench. The frames were temporary. They prevented landslides as workers built the permanent brick walls.

A brick arch joined the walls, and train tracks were laid on the tunnel's floor. Workers covered the entire structure with six feet (2 m) of soil. Then the roads were rebuilt above it.

AN EARLY SUCCESS

The first portion of the Underground, the Metropolitan Line, took just over three years to complete. It opened

Passengers were thrilled by test rides on the Metropolitan Line.

to passengers in January 1863. Most Londoners loved it immediately. They flocked to it to experience this new way of traveling under the city. In its first year, the Metropolitan Line carried 9.5 million passengers.

The success of the Underground generated excitement. In 1864, lawmakers received more than 250 proposals for adding to the railway. They approved plans to extend the Metropolitan Line. They also allowed railways to build new underground lines that circled the city.

The new lines were all built with the cut and cover method. But it soon became impractical. As London grew larger, its land grew more valuable. The cost of diverting sewers and digging trenches skyrocketed. It was too expensive to build more lines. But traffic was still bad.

THE GREATHEAD SHIELD

Civil engineer James Henry Greathead had an idea. He had improved upon early designs for a rectangular tunnel shield developed by Marc Isambard Brunel. Greathead's circular shield could bore tunnels without disturbing the roads above. It could also make deeper tunnels, so it was easier to avoid sewers. In 1886, Greathead began using his shield to build the Underground's City and South London Line.

The first step was to create a large, deep shaft. It allowed workers to get to the depth where the tunnel would be dug. Then the shield was placed into the shaft. The shield was a massive metal cylinder. The front had 16 steel blades to loosen the soil. Six hydraulic rams pushed the shield forward slowly.

MARC ISAMBARD BRUNEL

Engineers of the London Underground relied heavily on the work of a man named Marc Isambard Brunel. He invented the tunneling shield. Brunel used it to tunnel under London's River Thames. This tunnel opened in 1843. It was the first tunnel in the world to run under a body of water. Today's modern tunnel-boring machines can trace their origins to early tunneling shields.

Workers stood in the shield. They shoveled out the soil loosened by the blades. With the soil removed, workers installed cast iron plates. These formed a ring that became the tunnel walls. The result was a tube-shaped tunnel. Its circular shape was strong. It could withstand heavy loads from all sides.

For the City and South London Line, Greathead built two tunnels. Each carried trains moving in opposite directions. The size of these tunnels was much smaller than the cut and cover tunnels. Each of Greathead's tubes was approximately 10 feet (3 m) in diameter. The cut and cover tunnels were nearly twice that size.

ELECTRIC TRAINS

The small, deep tunnels could not use steam trains. They were too large to fit in the narrow tunnels. They would have no way to vent their smoke. Lawmakers approved a new type of train for Greathead's tunnels. Instead of steam, these trains used electricity.

THE GREATHEAD
SHIELD

The Greathead Shield was a massive piece of equipment. It was large enough for several people to work inside it. The conditions there were dark and wet. What advantages does the shield have over the cut and cover excavation method? Does it introduce any new dangers?

Rear View

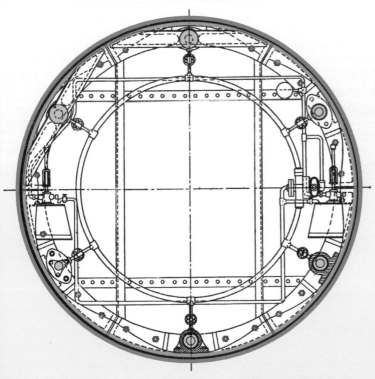

Side View

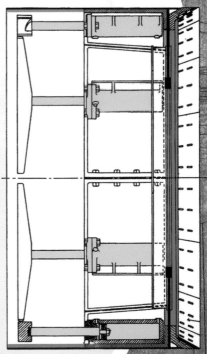

- Outer cylinder
- Blade guard
- Blades
- Hydraulic rams

An early electrical locomotive runs on the London Underground.

Electricity was a new technology that had not been widely used in trains. It would run through the tracks to power the trains. Venting would no longer be a problem because the electric trains did not give off smoke. Electric trains could also be made much smaller.

They did not need a huge boiler like steam trains. The small electric trains fit easily in the new, narrow tubes.

In 1890, the City and South London Line opened. It was the Underground's first deep tunnel line. It was also the world's first line to use electric trains. The result was a clean, fast way to travel across London. Parliament soon approved other deep electric lines. The Underground began to grow rapidly.

EXPLORE ONLINE

The London Underground is a feat of civil engineering. Bridges, tunnels, skyscrapers, and dams can be engineering marvels, too. Read the infographic at the link below that explains ten of the most impressive civil engineering projects. What do these projects have in common with the London Underground? How does civil engineering alter the way people live?

CIVIL ENGINEERING MARVELS

abdocorelibrary.com/engineering-london-underground

THE UNDERGROUND'S LEGACY

The Underground began as a form of transportation. But it quickly became much more than that. It influenced subway systems in other cities across the world. New suburbs sprang up next to its stations. Its tunnels even sheltered Londoners from bombs in times of war. Over many decades, the lines expanded and grew. New sections continue to be added today, more than 150 years after the London Underground first opened.

Over the decades, the expansion of the Underground influenced the development of the city around it.

HOUSING

Since its beginnings, the Underground has influenced where people in London live. The first line alone required more than 1,000 houses to be torn down. These homes were rundown and crowded. Their residents were often poor factory workers. More than 12,000 people were left homeless.

The railway companies built Underground stations on land outside the city. They encouraged the displaced residents to move there, where housing was less expensive. Then the people could ride the Underground to work every day.

This area near the Underground stations became known as Metroland. Its less expensive housing allowed many people to buy homes for the first time. They could get away from London's crowds, noise, and pollution. But they could still work in the city by traveling on the Underground.

Beck's simplified map style is still in use today.

A SYMBOL OF LONDON

As people moved out of London and into the suburbs, the lines kept expanding. By the 1930s, the map of the London Underground was full of snaking lines that were difficult to read. Harry Beck, an electrical engineer working for the Underground, came up with a new way to map the routes.

In 1931, Beck made a new, simplified map. He based it on the look of an electrical circuit diagram. Beck replaced the snaking lines with only vertical, horizontal, and diagonal lines. He emphasized where the lines crossed. Beck's improved map made the Underground easier to use. Today it is the basis for subway maps across the world. It is also a symbol of London.

THE ROUNDEL

The Underground has one of the world's most recognized logos. The design is a simple red ring known as the roundel. A blue bar with the word _underground_ printed on it sits on top of the roundel. It was first designed to stand out from other signs on buildings. But it has become more than that. It has become a symbol of the city itself.

PLACE OF SAFETY

The Underground had other influences on London as well. Its deep, thick-walled tunnels have sheltered London's citizens during war. The first time was during World War I (1914–1918), when Germany bombed London.

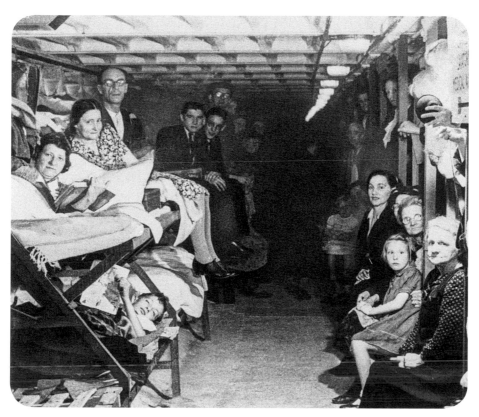

During World War II, Londoners sought shelter in the Underground's tunnels.

As sirens warned of attacks, people dashed into the Underground for safety.

During World War II (1939–1945), the Underground again saved many lives. Beginning in 1940, German airplanes bombed London heavily at night. Remaining at home was dangerous. Each night, Londoners went deep below ground to the safety of the tunnels.

The Underground had other uses in the war, too. Unfinished sections of tunnel were turned into factories. Workers there made parts for military airplanes. The prime minister, Winston Churchill, had a disused station converted into his bunker and office.

After the war, the Underground remained an important part of the city. New lines were built and older sections upgraded. Today, the Underground has 270 stations. Its 11 lines have 250 miles (402 km) of track. Without them, London would come to a standstill.

PERSPECTIVES
SECURITY

Although the Underground has been a place of safety, it has also been a target for violence. On July 7, 2005, terrorists planted three bombs in the Underground. Another bomb was planted on a bus above ground. When the bombs exploded, 52 people died. It was the worst-ever act of terrorism on British soil to date. In the years since the attack, the security on the Underground has increased. It has more than 700 police officers, 12,000 security cameras, improved lighting, and help stations.

MOVING INTO THE FUTURE

Today's passengers want more than just transportation. Riders expect modern comforts. Stations now offer Wi-Fi. Trains have air conditioning. Riders can receive real-time alerts about delays and closings. A service called the Night Tube provides 24-hour access to many lines. New signaling systems keep down delays. All of these upgrades ensure that the world's first underground railway is still one of its most impressive.

FURTHER EVIDENCE

Chapter Four discusses the London Underground's influence on the city in the last 150 years. What was one of the main points in the chapter? Read the opinion piece at the link below. Does the information in the article support one of the main points of the chapter? Give examples to support your opinion.

THE LONDON UNDERGROUND: STILL THE PEOPLE'S RAILWAY

abdocorelibrary.com/engineering-london-underground

FAST FACTS

- The London Underground was the world's first subway system.

- London's clay soil is the ideal place to build a tunnel because it is relatively easy to dig, but it is strong enough to keep from collapsing on itself.

- Laborers called navvies dug the Underground's first tunnels by hand using shovels and pickaxes.

- The earliest Underground lines were shallow and sat just a few feet below the street.

- The improved design of a tunnel shield led to deep-level tunnels.

- Electric trains eliminated the unpleasantly smoky stations caused by steam trains.

- Building Underground stations directly outside of London encouraged the growth of suburbs and allowed many people to become homeowners for the first time.

- During World Wars I and II, Londoners used the Underground as bomb shelters.

- The Underground's logo and map have become symbols of London.

- Today's Underground has many new features that appeal to modern-day riders, such as Wi-Fi, digital reports on delays, and all-night services.

- Approximately 1 billion people ride the London Underground each year.

43

STOP AND
THINK

Say What?

Engineering has many specific terms to describe forces, machines, and methods. Find three engineering terms in the book that you did not know. Look them up in a dictionary or the glossary, and write their definitions in your own words.

Surprise Me

Chapter Two examines the elements engineers had to think about before building the London Underground. Which of these elements surprised you the most? Why?

Take a Stand

Mass transit systems such as the London Underground are expensive to build, maintain, and staff. They can be unreliable, crowded, or dirty. But mass transit systems can also move thousands of people efficiently and cheaply. Do you think investing in a new mass transit system is wise for growing cities? Why?

You Are There

Imagine you got to ride on the London Underground on opening day. Write a letter to your friend detailing the sights, sounds, and smells you experienced. Were you scared? Was it like you expected it to be?

GLOSSARY

asphyxiation
a lack of oxygen that can lead to death

bore
to make a hole by drilling or digging

commuter
a person who travels back and forth to work regularly

divert
to switch from one path to another

elevated
raised above the ground

excavate
to dig out and remove soil and rock

hydraulic
powered by water or other fluid pressure

intercom
a communication system that uses microphones and speakers

main
a major pipe that carries a utility, such as gas or water

Parliament
the British government body that creates laws

shaft
a hollow, vertical cylinder that extends below ground level

termini
the last stations of a railway line

ventilation
a system of providing fresh air

ONLINE RESOURCES

To learn more about the London Underground, visit our free resource websites below.

Visit **abdocorelibrary.com** for free Common Core resources for teachers and students, including vetted activities, multimedia, and booklinks, for deeper subject comprehension.

Visit **abdobooklinks.com** for free additional online weblinks for further learning. These links are routinely monitored and updated to provide the most current information available.

LEARN MORE

McCarthy, Cecilia Pinto. *Engineering the NYC Subway System*. Minneapolis, MN: Abdo, 2018.

Sandler, Martin W. *Secret Subway*. Washington, DC: National Geographic, 2009.

INDEX

About the Author

Kate Conley has been writing nonfiction books for children for nearly two decades. When she's not writing, Conley spends her time reading, sewing, and solving crossword puzzles.